IN THE BLUE HOUR

JOHN SCARBOROUGH

IN THE BLUE HOUR

Coverstory books

First published in paperback format by
Coverstory books, 2025

ISBN 978-1-0684498-7-1

Copyright © John Scarborough, 2025

The cover image uses a photograph of Alcock
Tarn taken by the author.

www.coverstorybooks.com

Contents

It was the blue hour of life…where the world and the soul seemed to touch

(Carl Jung — "Memories, Dreams, Reflections")

These fragments I have shored against my ruins

(T. S. Eliot – "The Waste Land")

No Country for an Old Man

He keeps a young man's desire
buried alive, longs for rain to clear
the dust from his few distractions.

He lives alone in the blue hour,
somewhere between day and night,
gazing through darkness to luminous skies.

Memories return in borrowed light,
celluloid flickers through the gloom:
a child running, a lover's eyes.

In between, his riddle of pain,
CT scans, waiting rooms, just-warm tea;
age, both gift and impediment.

Yeats wished for eternity in Byzantium,
imagined a golden bough for his soul,
detached from an ailing body.

This man asks for one more Spring,
to play and sing and love again,
then death, like a falling leaf.

Alcock Tarn

In the minute before sunset
your breath stirs the tarn

>   flies sketch out their lives
>   on an eddy's updraught

lambs, touched by your artist's brush,
burn in the low water light

>   wind ripples glide to the mouth
>   in a silent dream-dance

where water spills
through stiffening lips

>   in silt swirls,
>   free falling glitter pearls.

As if she knew, the sun leaves,
catching our surprise.

A Rare and Precious Thing

An unexpected storm
hurls rain against the window,
hesitant droplets

cling to the glass,
blur the view of fields and trees
until ragged and vague

then give up and fall,
gently braid
each small pane.

Leaves, spears of grass,
move to the contours
of wind.

You pace backwards
to scrutinise
the first brush-strokes

of the morning,
oils still moist from
yesterday's hard-fought hours.

Those wild curls
are growing back,
a little darker.

You begin again
with vermillion,
ask only for another day.

Denial

The nurse
in her blue uniform,
knew death was coming,

she offered
a few extra words
like *metastasis* and *palliative*.

You chose *denial*,
entered your less desolate self,
a candle free to burn.

The disease travelled
by stealth on a slipstream
of faulty genes.

Obdurate, brutal,
a plundering
of breast, liver and lung.

You held on,
where not even love
could penetrate

and left
as a few droplets
put out the flame.

Brass Padlocks

on the old bridge, lovers' vows:
to the moon and back, Kerry and Kirk
together forever, Brenda and Rob

loops of silk ribbons along a wire
suggest a contradiction

pink forget-me-not spills
across the path to a wooden café,
open a lifetime ago

under ancient trees,
the applause of morning rain

the river bubbles over blunt stones,
eddies around fallen deadwood,
saplings jostle for air and light

a kindness felt in the litter
of last year's leaves

rain clears and the river slows,
offers its specular skin;
ashes are heavier than I imagine.

Last Fall
for Kathy

I can still see you under Sour Milk Ghyll,
in a quiet field where the Herdwick graze,
saying hello to strangers in kagoules,
oblivious to the darkening skies.

Falling water carries a welcome sound,
gentle now, a massage on softened stone;
where ferns burn to rust in the dying sun,
a stream glints by with a truth of its own.

How casually cloud-fog steals the peak
and claims the last flush of exhausted oak,
how readily the fallen leaves retreat
to cooling earth, impatient for snow's peace.

This perfect symmetry of winter's end
allowing sleep to come, like a lost friend.

Returning Alone to Glebe Farm

"The smallest sprout shows really there is no death" — *Walt Whitman*

How a place welcomes you
can feel like love.
It could be the massing of clouds
holding back a storm
from acre upon acre of wheat,
or the plainsong of wind
that carries you along a stoney path.
It could be the promise
of fire on a frosty night,
or the squeak of your garden gate.

How can you understand its affection?
You are here, now; beyond this place
everything feels incomplete.
This is where absence is filled,
where you have loved,
where your life is held, in these fields,
in the walls and floors of your home.
It is in the ripening grain,
each leaf of grass,
your neighbours waving hand.

Self-Portrait

Barely visible until you look closer,
between the bookcase with its spill

of art and poetry, a dog-eared Kavanagh,
the plays of Sean O'Casey

and her photo at dusk on Lough Neagh
with its frosted cape of naked trees,

a frame, the colour of old milk, its centre
a small rectangle of polished pewter

bearing the hand-painted letters 'gra',
a Gaelic word for love, used less now.

Fulcrum

I must leave you now
let go
the sadness
that dries my bones
or I will fall
without resistance
as dust to hard floor
swept up
in the passing days
of your absence.

I need to go
where loneliness
can begin
where I am anonymous
to all things
except the rain
where pavements and trees
are new and wet
and the morning
calls me again.

Silence

Today, I received an invitation.
Alone in your room, it seems
the invitation has been extended:

your father's oak desk
scratched like a map,

stacked books, their quiet pages,
your easel in the corner,
brushes in a jar.

I enter its circumference,
where only my breathing
disturbs the air.

I consider an unfamiliar
question: is there anything worth
leaving here for?

First Year

adrift on the sea's skin
not even a zephyr's murmur
stars   a blade of moon
suffocate in cloud
at the curve   flashes of dawn
return my questions
like morse code
again and again and again
how to sail the distance
how to navigate clashing rocks

Automat
(Edward Hopper 1927)

Forgive the intrusion but I can see
you too are familiar with the night.
No-one calls you home; you sit alone
in the built absence of *Automat*.

I am drawn to your porcelain face,
that un-gloved hand I imagine
will tremble as you lift
the warmed cup to your lips.

I too have felt the city's critique,
the cold comfort of solitude.
You remind me I am not alone,
a brief anchor in a tranquil place.

I have studied you closely,
though I cannot guess your regret
or suppose our separate lives
are bound by a mirrored light.

I have no part in your film noir.
There is no shared denouement,
despite the lure of painted lips,
or an afterthought of red apples.

Woman at the Bar

The woman at the bar
is wearing a leopard skin print,
black and white,
like a snow cat.
She turns to look at me
but it's too late,
I already know it's not you.

On Reflection

A day like any other
but for the quality of light.
I stare into the bathroom mirror

at an unfamiliar self:
a face, now creased and grey,
eyes with no hint of curiosity.

An unnerving likeness
to my father staring back at me.
Where is that younger man

who played Alice Cooper's
School's Out at full volume
during the end of term speech

who set off for adventure
with a framed rucksack
feathered hair and ninety quid

who shared a rite of passage with
Anna from Malmo, all the way
from Brussels to Brindisi

from Piraeus to Mykonos
with its clear and salty sea, to float,
rudderless, under a cobalt sky?

Fire in the Trees

Six o' clock
the sun poised,
slant light
burns a rowan's leaves.

Eyes shut
against the glare,
heat rushes me
like a zealous lover.

I think of us together
in long grass,
thighs locked, laughing
until our stomachs hurt.

Each new depression
chokes the sun,
monotone hangs dull
on the branch.

I want to feel
every leaf ignite again,
open my eyes
to fire in the trees.

Tell me, what remains
but the thrill
of recalled love.

Escape

Across a quiet road to the gap in drystone
with its damp clots of velvet green,
down the stone steps to a wooden bridge

that straddles a flickering stream,
a welcome on the edge-light of dawn,
the dewy air cool against my skin

urging a quicker pace to Rydal Water,
the crunch of fine gravel at the shore,
leaping over boulder-rock, cold splatters

against the legs, my calves' stiff response
to the heavy slap of Vibram soles,
breathing deeper now, climbing the terrace

heart pumping in high gear, blood and air
burning arteries, until a quiet cadence
is found along a path to Loughrigg

where eyes can rest on the distant lake,
turning at a gate to the woods,
coasting downhill, scent of early Spring

the welcome of last year's fallen leaves:
oak, larch, sycamore and lime kick up
and tickle the shins; faster now

along the tarmac road to a lakeside café
boats for hire and home-made scones
where faerie folk were known to roam

to the grey slate of Grasmere village
with its rooms for walkers and tourists,
busy buttering their morning toast

across the 592, to finish with a sprint past
Dove Cottage, salute the poet, call out,
The loveliest spot that man hath ever found!

A Borrowed Feast

(After "The Shepherd's Life" — James Rebanks)

I have no claim to this land
of fells, fields, hedges, and ghylls,
of woods, paths and lanes.
I have never tamed a stream,
or built a drystone wall.

Neither farmer nor shepherd,
I am ignorant of fell-gathering,
or clearing out the higher crags,
of intakes, mule hogs, flystrike,
or smit marks on the backs of lambs.

I have only a pair of timeworn boots,
to climb this rain-polished shoulder
to its airy ridge, stand at the peak,
feast on our incalculable world.

As lights from scattered homes
draw down the night,
I return to the valley's quiet
under settled cloud, no wind,
just a few sighs to turn the leaves.

Tien Shan
(Heavenly Mountains)

From a narrow ledge, the roar
of a green river

rising through a sun-lit wall
of heat.

Cloudless, an eagle circles
above ragged peaks.

Cool Hand Luke films our roped
ascent, 800 metres

scalds the lungs, strains metal
and bone, until

we reach a bareness of rock,
jagged and crystalline.

Francesca scatters the ashes
of a mountaineer

Sean lays a bog-cotton flower,
whispers a prayer.

Others boil water for tea, swap
stories from home:

five o'clock traffic, power cuts,
evening rain.

For some, this was more difficult.
Tien Shan has levelled us.

Lost

Later in the Lamb Inn
two northern lads square off
over a plate of pie and peas.
*You don't know your arse
from your elbow*,
says the bald one with the map
and mud on his knees.
Weren't me that got us lost,
says the thin one,
dripping in his drink.

Two pints of Theakston's later,
no-one notices
as the volume is turned up;
they're too busy
telling their own tales
of a compass that lies,
of maps that are crap,
of rain, wind and fog
on the fells…
Ay up, says the bald one,
a bit red-faced,
Where's the bloody dog?

Christmas Eve

Dusk falls in the valley,
enters the trees, binds the geometry
of roofs, chimneys, spires,
before a summoning of distant lights.

A river's ceaseless course
carries the day-long hours to the sea,
leaving peace here, nights prayer
calming a city's insistent pulse.

The River Welcomes Strangers

Walking the bank at first light,
grey-green water,
flashes of silver
between charcoal sketches
of winter trees.

I am a stranger here, like all my fathers
in need of comfort:
the timeless greeting
of its ceaseless flow, preordained,
towards the ocean.

Others locked in their own circles
of light and shadow
return each day
to feel its current and rhythm,
its gravity.

Women and men in slender boats
bow and sweep
where swans drift past;
gulls, their grey wings and white breasts,
kiss the river's skin.

The Oarsman and the Swan

Inhale,
he leans and dips,
the river as glass

Exhale,
he pulls and lifts,
waves of crystal break.

In the camouflage
of reeds
a pair of mute swans
have built their Spring home.

The cob glides
into the quiet light

purest white,
as if he drank from a secret well
or lived on a diet of pearls.

The oarsman,
an old friend of the river,
twists his torso,
eyes the swan

who lifts a lofty neck,
curls back,
arches titan wings.

The boat drifts closer,
the cob prepares to charge

yet hesitates…
perhaps a memory
of kindness stills him.

The oarsman understands
his trespass,
pulls hard on single oar,
rows to the far bank

where the sun loiters
and the river is unhurried.

A Small Triumph
For Sam

Wisps of cirrus were still and gave no clue
to the wild, mocking wind about to blow
off the North Sea, that day in October.
Each in turn, grandad, father and brother
lift their arms, release, pull hard on the line.
A sideways sweep, a few ungainly spins
before the flimsy bundle spirals down,
to crash and quiver on the rigid ground.

Then you, the youngest child, at last allowed
to take the strain, let go as fresh wind sends
the kite soaring to a speck in the cloud,
where you guide it with strong and steady hands,
gently swaying and drawing on taut strings,
a puppet master to an eagle's wings.

A Sense

        rising with the morning,
in voices
above the clink of metal;
in blue striped awnings,
still life displays of apples, bananas, plums,
turnips, caulies and cut flowers;
in the first shout of a costermonger
echoing through history

        as early mist burns;
in sunlight flashes
on the Mason Arms,
a smell of bacon in the pan
and dark-roast coffee from the stall
on Little Butcher Lane;
in waves of bunting
between

        a huddle
of Georgian buildings;
in the taste of onion bhaji,
or lemon tart baked by skinny girls
raising cash for skinnier refugees;
in listening to a busker's sad songs,
or the toll of church bells
at each passing hour;

        in unknown faces,
bright, winter bobble hats,
catching up with gossip
at the soft borders between old and young;
in found spaces of intimacy;
in the perseverance of an old man,
his pot leg tapping across tarmac
to ask after Mandy's bad hips;

in the first sale,
the next and the next;
in fretting for those missing: the bookseller,
a gap at the top of the square;
in enquiries made
and assurances given;
a sense of something,
to reconcile us with the world.

Aftermath: the Liminal World of Francesca and Tomasch

Francesca prepares the olives
in a garlic marinade,
scented with fresh coriander.
She serves them in the blue glaze
of earthenware pots,
draws a pitcher of water
at the *fuente* where children
unspool their lives.

At the stone house bistro,
voices, laughter again,
the smell of *guisado*.
In the light of whitewashed walls,
a young couple play cards,
her loose blouse a distraction;
leaves on the sacred oak quiver
in shifting air.

The first family return,
una mesa para tres por favor.
Tomasz fingerpicks his guitar:
he remembers the dead,
but his song is for the living,
the lovers and the mourners.
His song is a prayer
and he prays, he prays.

Post-Mortem

The scene from above
I would expect
at this time of year

the lawn neatly mown,
soil dark from watering,
borders cut square

a boast of colour:
honeysuckle, aquilegia,
a climbing rose.

Under the apple trees,
in mottled shade,
a woman I once loved

rhythmically sweeps away
the June-drop
of unwanted fruit.

On the washing line,
new silk lingerie
caught by a fresh breeze.

Fault Lines

He is reading Homer,
an old scholar's obsession.
She lifts crystal to her lips,
an early lover's gift.

His hand turns the page,
hers tilts the glass.

Wisps of hair
fall on heavy frames,
his eyes are dulled by obscurities,
his skin aches for sunlight.

In a vision from his book,
he is waiting at the shore,
his questions threaten
to fracture air.

But he has never carried a sword,
nor braved the rough seas,
he has led a surrogate life
in study halls.

Beneath the lace covered table,
her red shoes.

The Old Masters
(After "Musée Des Beaux Arts" — W H Auden)

About suffering, according to Auden,
the Old Masters were never wrong.
They knew its human condition.

In a resort-town Intensive Care,
blood cells and pathogens skirmish
through a grandfather's pumped lungs.

Nurses and doctors in flimsy armour
line his bed, wait for the count,
lift him, turn him, chest down.

Across fields on the edge of town,
Ploughmen are tilling the rich soil,
as fine as a girl's braided hair.

Dogs running free are still
doing their doggy business,
sheep are fat with unborn lambs.

The tides still follow the moon
and sunlight washes the waves,
whether or not the tourists come.

In the distance, giant turbines
circle slowly, murmur on the breeze,
heard only by a solitary hawk.

Spring Watch

In her blue pinafore she opens the oven
to a slap of heat, checks the browning skin,
and whispers, *only a few minutes more.*

Outside, not really a garden, a back yard,
washing line over a path to the shed,
the smell of old wood and metal.

Turned with a fork in November's damp,
you plant a dozen bulbs in a modest
shock of soil, forgotten until today.

Now, sitting on a bench, racing pages
on your lap, you gaze above imagined
winners until the first calyx unzips.

Hardly a blink as yellow petals
unfold against an old brick wall,
trumpets of daffodils bursting through.

How patient you seem to a small boy,
watching you from the window,
so still, in your silvered cage.

Coffee With Grandad

I swear if I gaze long enough
in the new coffee shop window
at the corner of Marshall's Yard,
I see my grandad's face,
creased and smeared with oil,
staring back at me.

I figured it out the other day.
Where the young barista
lines up coffee cups,
steams skinny latte,
must be the exact spot
my grandad's patterns were cut.

White hot cylinders of light
poured from clanking steel,
filling all angles and corners
of the mould before plunging
into the fog of the cooling pit
with a deafening *SHUSSHH.*

Sometimes, when I can silence
the chatter, the clinking of cups,
I hear the sirens call
to end the twilight shift,
bacon fat crackles in the pan,
boots scrape on the passage floor.

Gold Watch and a Badge

An empty sleeve
tucked in a broad leather belt.
The white silk
of your hair.

Sunday visits:
barely a word spoken
as you slice ham or cake
with your special blade.

Years later,
I suppose an error
when I inherit
a gold-plated pocket watch

for thirty years' service
in the foundry
of a small
Midlands town

and to counter
those white feather girls,
a silver-plated
War Badge

for a year
and eighty-six days,
until the order
for the Big Push

where shrapnel
found you.
I imagine a teenager
waiting in the Field Hospital

for hot tea, perhaps a cigarette
and skilled hands;
my unknowing
preserved in your silence.

To a Father
(Extracted from completed army forms and correspondence sent to my great grandfather during WW1)

Sir,
I regret to inform you that a report
has this day been received from the War office
to the effect that 31291, private JS
was wounded in action on 23rd October 1916
at a place unstated.

I have just arrived at the hospital.
(The name and place of the hospital
are not to be filled in by the soldier)

If the soldier is in a grave condition
the Medical Officer in Charge is authorised
to issue a free railway warrant to one relation.

Description on leaving the Colours:
(to prevent impersonation)
Age: 20 years 27 days
Height: 5 ft 7 inches
Complexion: Fair
Eyes: Blue
Hair: Brown

Trade as stated by him on enlistment:
Butcher.

A solemn, steady, and well-behaved man
in the service of his country.

Marks or scars
whether on the face or other parts of the body:
Loss of right arm

Discharged in consequence of being
no longer physically fit for war.

In the event of any doubt, description and signature
should be carefully compared with present
appearance and handwriting.

War Badge awarded
For "Services Rendered" in H.M.'s Military Forces
For 1 year, 86 days.

Recruiting rewards will be paid to recruiting agents
for each recruit raised:
2s. 6d. to 5s. Regular Army.

Nymphéas

"Your paintings…will serve as a reminder of peace in a world that has known too much war." George Clemenceau, French Prime Minister 1917-1920

Monet's hymn to nature,
painted as a bird sings,
in semi-breves of blue,
in descending minims of yellow,
each fleeting note bound
to elements of light, water and air

an offer to sublimate
the battle-cries of war
a century ago,
from soldiers who died
in the blood-pools
of horizonless fields.

Rhythms of colour and light
enter and rest in the mind's eye;
out of the mud,
these delicate Nymphéas float,
their haunting beauty,
weightless and free.

Five Days
(for Irina Gen)

A language teacher from Penza
takes a hammer to propaganda.
She dares to question.

It begins in a village kindergarten.
Children lie flat in tricolour Z formation.
In secondary schools, Pavlik is resurrected

to listen and whisper from hushed rooms.
Most kids remain silent, await their passage
under a symbol of scarlet sails.

It's an old story, retold.
If you don't believe there's a war,
there isn't.

On TV screens and social media,
the viscera of smashed buildings,
bodies abandoned in the streets.

With no objective lens, we magnify images
fashioned in the mind's eye.

The teacher looks East and West,
fears silence in the Motherland
more than the latest Archipelago.

It takes five days for the summoning
before a curtain falls.

That Bloody Book
("1984" — George Orwell)

The prisoner in your charge
steps aside to avoid a puddle
on his way to the gallows. Still alive!

Light fades over Sea of the Hebrides,
Black Jagg roll-ups fug the room
inhaled through infected lungs.

You sit to write, the first crimson specks
caught in a laundered handkerchief,
death counting each laboured breath.

You resist, as in those long winters,
wrapped in an old coat, recording
the poor and the dispossessed

in mud-bound trenches
where seeds of betrayal germinate
and a sniper's bullet finds your throat.

You resist, the wounded elephant
who won't die, until your agony is complete,
until *that bloody book* is written.

To warn the world
of what it is capable.

An Extraordinary, Ordinary Man
i.m. Malcolm Stringer

We met across a low brick wall
between terraced homes,
each with a narrow strip of soil.

He was younger then, fixed his own
house, eased the stiffness
in doors swollen by hard rain.

He was strong, impressive, bushy
beard and Yorkshire brogue,
gentle as a winter moon.

A theologian, who listened
to an earthly call, quit his pulpit
to serve those who broke the law.

He found them at the margins:
squats, HIMO's, half-way hostels,
shared floors and prison cells.

Some understood, felt his worth,
others labelled him a social worker
for the least deserving poor.

He was a family man, an old Volvo,
double bass in a skiffle band,
the vinyl in a Black Box stereo.

He was laughter in a bar,
footprints on the moorland fells,
a man at ease as he passed by.

Conversations in a Day Centre (1988)

Mary-Jane who liked vodka,
a big bloke known as Bull
and a lad with a tattooed neck
called Jack
who scared everyone.

Each day (except weekends)
the rootless walked in
for a hot drink and a smoke
to chat   or just sit
minding their own.

Some were violent   others
would steal to get by
most had slipped
through broken nets.

Social workers   educated
soft shoes
stone wash denim
picked at their lives
from steel chairs

with red fabric seats
and cigarette burns
took notes
at low-set tables
Formica tops and ash trays

wiped clean at 5 o'clock
as the rootless walked out
looking for a bed
a floor   a shop door
or another town.

Saplings

An island of grass in the centre
of the estate, whips of birch
tied to wooden posts and a sign:
All ball games prohibited, by Order.
Raymond kicks a ball against windows
until its seams burst; I help him,
we love the sound of shattering glass.
A year later, Saint Paul's Communion plate
is missing, Raymond becomes a Borstal Boy
and a ten-pound ticket to New Zealand
uproots the Jackson kids.

Dad works weekends, buys a plot
in a village, miles from town.
I can still see burning grass, flames
higher than me, blue lights;
Raymond would have liked that fire.
Three years to build a new home
in white bricks, pure white: polished floors,
a study lined with *Reader's Digest* books,
goal-posts in a garden with trees.
It's 1968, most days after school
I pretend to be George Best.

The Invitational Edge

He fell through his mother's loose hands so he's taken away by a woman in red shoes who never stops smiling until they reach a three-storey house with a steel fence and apple trees in the front garden where a softly spoken man offers him lemonade then explains he'll be staying for a while in the attic room with an older boy called Raymond who lays out a silver plate and three silver goblets from St Jude's which must to be dumped as soon as 'cos he can't sell them to Concrete Eddie who usually offers him decent money for silver stuff and even more for gold which is hard to get hold of in this part of town but since wheels are so simple to hot-wire Raymond makes a promise to show him all his tricks tomorrow when they have to do chores for bed-and-board like clearing out weeds or collecting fallen apples 'cos it's dead easy to bunk off and take a Fiesta or maybe a Golf GTI for a blast over Bleak Low and burn it in a field by the side of Old Coach Road.

The Boy in the Doorway

Mid-winter in the historic quarter,
the last restaurant closing as I step out
to freezing air; barely a blade of moon,
church spires lamping the night sky.

A rag-pile on damp cardboard,
a statistic, invisible on the dark street
but for a face, framed in old newsprint
and a blue bobble hat.

He can't be more than sixteen, this boy,
lying in the doorway of Café Zoot,
who flinches at my approach, weighs risk,
eyes as sharp as a hunted cub.

Knowing a warm hotel is a minute away,
I remove a woollen coat,
offer a lifeline, I suppose, at minus five;
he hesitates, then repeats *thank you, thank you.*

I leave him in the shadows,
walk on through a Roman arch,
where a magnificent cathedral is lit up,
like Gabriel's wings.

To Siobhan

In my version, you never stand
in the dock, leaning on bandaged arms
towards an old man in a red robe.

You don't enter your father's room
at three am, full of drink, to check if he
sleeps, can't ask yourself once more

if the devil has finally left him.
You don't pour spirit on crumpled
bedsheets, strike and toss a match

watching it flare through the dark,
ignite a blue wall of flame across his body.
In my version, you never close

the door, walk outside to sit alone
against the brick wall of the house,
or begin to think of yourself as free.

You haven't cut yourself diagonally,
a tallying on each of your wrists,
like a prisoner's calendar.

The Defendant

Dad died today,
or was it yesterday, or the day before?
They never told me.
Mum's wearing her new blue dress

I stole from White Stuff. Easy.
Please Mum, come and visit me,
now you're better.
I miss you.

They strapped my arms.
So I've seven cuts on my right arm,
six on the other.
When it's over, I'll need a blade.

They're all staring, especially the judge,
who looks angry, like he did.
The social worker's all dressed up;
my lawyer looks funny in a wig.

Nobody knows me, or him;
they think they do.

Saturday night, as regular as Mass,
I can still smell the whiskey on his breath,
see his bony cheeks when I strike a match.

It's my birthday today;
he bought me a Barbie doll once.
A month for every year
would be alright.

The Judge

An infant taken in his nanny's arms,
public schoolboy, lover, Oxbridge scholar.
Now, in his fifth age, he is Justice,
and will play his part.

His leading role endorsed by a horse-hair crown
and scarlet robe, he perches at his bench,
faces an assembled cast: lawyers, clerks, police;
the audience in the gallery, quiet.

He can see bandages on the Defendant's arms,
a bruise above her left eye;
her plea invites an act of retribution,
punishment that her pain cannot mitigate.

He listens to each actor in turn,
arguments for and against the accused,
sees neither virtue nor harmony here,
only the right or the wrong of it.

The judge looks down from his bench
at a girl in the dock, who may not speak.
Outside, snow settles on grey pavements,
cars move slowly through the main street.

Man on a Beach

in a canvas chair,
between dunes that call him
and the possessive sea

he waits for high tide
as the sun completes
its low arc

decades earlier,
a boy roams the highs and lows
of blown sand

to hear collapsing waves,
the shriek of gulls,
the silence of dunes

lost in his imaginings;
no need for friends
or a mother to call him home

now at twilight,
turbines trace zero circles
across the sky

he watches a sandpiper
quick-step through foam;
counts the hours and days alone

tide flows cool over his toes;
gentler against his thighs,
his shoulders.

Ribblehead Viaduct, Autumn 1869

Catch a flash of sepia
over tea in the station café,
you're a hundred feet high
in a mesh of scaffold planks,
bent to a funnelled wind
that flicks them up and down
like piano keys.

Bore through struts and rails
to Archibald Mattinson,
thorax crushed by a wagon
of black limestone,
now the star turn
at St Leonard's this Sunday

where the minister barters
penance and prayers
for a slice of heaven,
and at days end you too
can follow the bull's eye
lanterns to Sebastopol.

a roof over your head
a meal at your table
a coat on your back

Aubade

On his first morning of death,
it seems he is lost to the blue light

but grief is a curious friend;
here, at his mooring, all things leave a trace:

this claw hammer hung on a nail,
its rubber handle worn from his grip and swing

the smell of oil and old tools,
a litter of blonde shavings, damp rags for linseed

this hand-saw in the vice, sharp from the file,
the grin and glint of it

as he pushed and pulled its length
across a grain of oak or elm

and his old bench with so many failing joints,
salt and grit holding them together.

First Touch

According to the young surgeon,
your heart was an empty Tesco bag
and a clot had stolen your voice.

I had grown used to the distance
between us. It was seeing you lying
mute in a hospital bed.

I had no memory of touching you.
I held a callused hand, felt warm skin
over loose bones.

You didn't object to the lavender oil,
which surprised me, nor to my first
hesitant strokes:

the circles I drew on your thighs,
the gentle flexing of feet and toes,
the slow release of a knotted calf.

It was too late for resolution;
perhaps the most we could hope for
was the beginning of forgiveness.

I can see you now, on a distant roof,
hammering and sawing the rafters,
your back bronzing in the midday sun.

Tow Rope

My father laid down his claw hammer,
took a rope from his truck

and lashed me to a chimney stack
on a half-nailed roof.

Nine jets in diamond pattern
roared over a boy's dizzy head

until they broke, to a starburst
in blue, white and red.

On glass at the edge of dawn,
we fished for roach and silver bream;

quietly, as if in prayer,
I watched him, for the slightest quiver.

When I made the school six,
he carved a chess set in American oak.

On the eve of my eighteenth,
he wept; sorry we hadn't been close.

A year or so later, he hung on to the rope
when the old truck was sold.

The End of Something

The riving shed is silent:
saws, benches, rollers and rails
stripped by the owners,
plundered like a boneyard.

It stands on buckled legs,
corrosion feeds on its frame.
Boarded windows fade to yellow,
as if sodium lights were left on

to keep alive a history
that offers only its hollow stare.
A few illusionary fragments
in the debris of skilled men.

Here is beauty in slow decay,
where scars texture memory
and death defers its purpose
until the final day, hour, minute.

'The Loneliness Thing Is Overdone'
(Edward Hopper)

Dusk, the last car passed by an hour ago
heading out for the sunshine coast;
a man at the roadside locks the pumps,
wipes down the bright red paintwork.
Soon he'll switch off a neon-lit Pegasus,
walk the line to his room on the lot.
In forty years, he's never left the state.
He likes glossy pictures in *Life* magazine:
big city skyscrapers, Yellowstone,
the blue-green Pacific; he dreams up
open road adventures in a cream Cadillac,
marking every stop on the company map.
He had the chance of a ride to California,
Okies in a pick-up, desperate for gas,
but too many dust-bowlers came back,
broken, half-starved, drained of faith.
He offers old tyres, a rest room, hope.
Best of all, he likes the long evenings,
nothing but the wind's song in the trees.

Seven A.M. 1948
(Edward Hopper)

("The morning seems to have no light to spare" — J. Hollander)

Perhaps Hopper's intention is to reveal an incongruence
of form and shape between shop and forest,
an unwanted trespass on the landscape;
this cube of clapboard, paint and glass,   ·
steals the morning light, as if by divine right.

It stands at the edge of the natural world, vacant and alone,
as if the artist understands our human position.
Perhaps it's too early to open, or is time suspended?
No one looks out from the windows, no one looks in,
those native trees holding the darkness.

Life Stilled – Hockney's World

We stand with the artist
at the boundary of his linear home,
a palisade in geometric blue.

Beyond V lines of cactus pots,
a half-view of lake or pool,
palette and texture unsettle
until the retina adjusts;
with new ways of seeing —
pink trees and patterned hills —
our eyes gorge on colour.

This could be Eden,
before the consummation,
when riverbeds were jewelled
and moths flew with luminous wings,
when earth was untainted
by human endeavour.

The real is reimagined,
and the reimagined
dilates the mind.
The offering here is not truth
but something
at least equal to it.

Indian Yellow

light that lingers
over tree and field
on September afternoons

as a lover's touch
rests in the memory

dying leaves
stubble wheat
a luminous moon

late summer's cloak
against the rising brume

Painted Boats, Annecy

Huddled each side of the river,
names like Papy and Veronique.

Each colour, shape, pattern
imagined in brushstrokes

cadmium yellow or ultramarine,
set against a distant iron bridge.

You had to record every angle,
as if we're in a painting by Seurat

arching trees, sun-flares,
families stretched along the bank.

We sat like children on the bridge,
legs dangling between rails

your last still shot rising
through emerald-clear water.

Brushstrokes
(Young Girl at a Window – Richard Glet)

What is it that makes
a young girl and an old woman
stand at a window full of yellow light?

Outside, faintly drawn buildings;
hidden from view — imagined traffic,
the quickening of other peoples' lives.

Light shines on the girl's dress,
the old woman wears
the room's purple shadows.

Brushstrokes stop the clocks,
allow us to witness
the quiet joy of the ordinary

the young girl with her grandmother,
after school, gazing on the city,
talking of small things.

We understand the light will change,
the looks, the silences,
their world of possibilities.

Making Up

night hours unnoticed
after the ceasefire

high tide's tracery
now moon-lit

you sleep, covers
rolled back in love's heat

pieces of moon
on your skin, breath

ebbing, flowing
in the room's memory

Legacy

My child will sit with her child
to gaze at this quiet river,
where old trees fill the horizon
and the sun cools at close of day.

She will explain, as she comes of age,
we expected reward for sacrifice,
for living small on this beautiful planet;
it was always here in the green fields.

Promiscuous with earth's gifts,
we demanded more and more,
indifferent to the sparrow's fall.
This calm water, trees in full leaf

are illusion, images recorded
from my life, when we failed her.

The Storm

People were swept through the streets,
stripped bare, for death or re-birth,
washed clean as pristine laundry.
The sun, in her melancholy, didn't care.

One of the old gods drew a circle
where a fossil might one day suggest life.
If you find me in a jewelled riverbed,
please, don't disturb my serenity.

+2.5°C

1. Prayer

Sand from the creeping Namib
blunts the bones of a goat's carcass.
Pearl millet and maize
lie burnt on the ground.

A farmer looks to the sky,
she prays for rain to fall
hard and loud
against make-shift troughs,
dry leaves, cracked riverbeds.

Some villagers have left
in search of a promised land.
But there's a rumour:
the ocean takes
what the desert spares.

Another world, in fear of itself,
is asking questions;
she tries to explain
to a stranger with blue eyes
and a microphone:

Without rain, we cannot plant.
Without rain, we cannot eat.
Without rain, we cannot drink.

2. Survival

In the Namib, a lone black beetle
flexes under her carapace,
crawls through a dry riverbed,
heat rising to the slack of day.

She crackles over hot sand,
climbs in folds of naked rock,
higher and higher until,
on spindle legs, she basks in fog
drifting in from the sea.

The beetle allows a cold drip
to braid her back, and drinks,
no more or less than she needs.

3. Diamonds

In the hot wind,
he watches each cow fall
until, among plains of nothingness,
all his diamonds are lost:

the unanchored soil,
children, not yet born,
running naked through the rain.

If Earth Could Tell Us

(Adapted from WH Auden's villanelle "If I Could Tell You")

Earth can do nothing but put on a show,
She doesn't know the price we have to pay;
If earth could tell us she would let us know.

If we should protest when flames are aglow,
If all the fish should scream in Arctic's grey,
Earth can do nothing but put on a show.

There is no vision of who will die, although,
Because life is more precious than we can say,
If earth could tell us, she would let us know.

Science has explained why hurricanes blow,
There are reasons given for the heat of clay;
Earth can do nothing but put on a show.

Perhaps the flowers really want to grow,
All living creatures intend to stay;
If earth could tell us, she would let us know.

Suppose the birds and bees decide to go,
Crops should fail and farmers walk away;
Can earth do nothing but put on a show?
If she could tell us, she would let us know.

A Candle in the Dark
(After Mahmoud Darwish)

a candle for the schoolteacher
who believes in you,
a candle for the nurse on a double shift
and for snow on blue cedar

a candle for the barista
who serves great coffee every time,
a candle for the soldier under fire
and for rain on wild orchids

a candle for 5am risers: posties, bakers,
swimmers who dream of Olympic glory,
a candle for the dad who always shows up
and for Large Blue butterflies

a candle for anyone who lives small
on our fragile planet,
a candle for those who must hide in shadows
and for each fallen leaf.

Resurrection

A new cycle begins, a team event:
blue on blue, the flower-heads of wild
thyme, colonies of complicit red ants.

A tale of the Large Blue butterfly,
extinct in England for decades,
resurrected by a miracle of science.

Blue eggs from the island of Öland,
a trail of Battenburg crumbs
and a patient professor in Oxford

unravel a butterfly's intricate cycle.
A story of tenacity, deceit, seduction,
a caterpillar's parasitic consumption

offers gifts of fairy-tale blue, flitting
across the grasslands of Somerset,
their dusky wings catching a June sky.

Note: Professor Jeremy A Thomas is credited with the return of the Large Blue butterfly, extinct since 1972.

Envy

If there is a route back from the grave,
I prefer to return as a blueberry.

It's those exquisite cloudy-blue coats,
their unique, silver-tongue texture.

In this life, I have never felt as cool
as a blueberry, nor have I been desired

for my distinguished looks or taste.
I am of limited benefit to humankind

no anti-oxidants or flavonoids here.
I could hardly be called a super anything.

If I was nurtured for a specific purpose,
fulfilling that purpose and nothing else

would render me a contented berry,
among friends, on a big blueberry bush

somewhere quiet with a view;
the Atlas Mountains or Ecuadorian Sierra.

Ode to Joy

A young girl offers coins and a smile
to a tall man with a double bass.

A woman in blue carries a cello
to a wooden chair, draws her bow.

The first bars of Beethoven's *Ninth*
wash through the square.

Senses dulled by the white noise
of a small-town piazza awake

some sway in time, others clasp hands
or simply stand, mesmerised.

A child climbs a painted streetlamp
to steal a better view.

Most smile; drift closer, drawn
to the slow bowing of hymnal melody.

As if tutored by Orpheus, the allegro
begins with violins, flute, French horn.

People dance, tap toes, wave their arms,
choral singers burst into song.

All other songs:
of desire,
of loss,
of sorrow
are silenced

as gates swing open to the fields of Elysium

Revision
(After Hugo Williams)

They've bunked off for the morning,
this couple sipping cappuccinos at a small table
in the low lights of Café Nero.
They wear the same crested sweatshirts.

She has written out revision cards
about the Spanish Civil War, he is testing her.
She struggles so he offers clues, in Spanish,
to boast his linguistic skills.

I know this, I know this, don't tell me, she protests.
He teases her with another hint:
he whispers the name Manuel Azana,
they both lean in, a little closer.

She has teenage spots, but he doesn't see them,
nor does he see the posters of elegant Italian
women or an old man sipping espresso
in the corner, thinking how lucky they are.

Here they can sit and enjoy each other,
under the camouflage of questions and clues,
allowing nervous laughter to fill a pause,
while behind their eyes, a fire burns.

From a Bench

Painted white, now blistered, and sun-dried,
the bench stands at the high point of the park,
in memory of the late Mary Joan Bishop

who (according to local gossip) sat here with
her thermos and notebook, above this sea
of mown grass, its islands of maple and lime

to watch townsfolk stroll along the stone
paths and imagine their lives in short stories
she would later submit to *The Strand Magazine*.

On this warm Sunday afternoon,
a silver-haired woman in a pink cotton dress,
yellow shawl and sandals, passes quietly by.

A late summer flower against the green,
she moves with all the grace her years allow,
carries a parcel tied and bowed in black satin.

I might suppose a gift for a friend who lives
in one of the Georgian cottages by the river,
or perhaps, something special for the gentleman

walking towards her, dressed in a blue linen
jacket, his golden retriever dragging
a tight lead, breathless in the sun-lit heat.

The January Tree

She is counting the folds in her skin,
'I'll give up chocolate,' she says, breathing in.

I am staring through cold glass at the January tree,
its bare wintry limbs black against the sky.

Perfect silhouette, a former self, lighter now,
allowing light to penetrate the room.

A new wind rattles, fracture lines open
across the glass, I see a last leaf dance.

Separate Lives

He wakes to pain
drilling into his shoulder blade,
to heavy showers against the window,
the hiss of tyres on a wet road.

He turns on his radio:
another village burns in Palestine,
a boat is missing in the channel,
this year's *Strictly* winner is a blind comedian.

Moss covers the neighbour's roof;
he hasn't seen her this morning,
just a gardener clearing the border,
carers coming and going.

Someone has lit a fire,
pale smoke rising from her chimney,
threading through the damp air
like the close of a Papal ceremony.

Her flowered curtains are still closed;
he wonders if she feels any pain,
if she listens to the radio,
to passing cars or the drum of rain.

In Praise of Sunflower Leaves

A halo of ray florets,
a vanity,
designed to steal the sun's yellow,
to seduce
the winged carrier,
yet it failed jealous Clytie,
rapt by the sun,
whose passion for Helios
still burns
in all her beauty.

Heart-shaped leaves,
rough as a cat's tongue,
vein and veinlet
sweating the day-long hours
to feed a mistress,
shedding all surplus rain,
each droplet
of water and light
falling away
like unstrung pearls.

*Note: In Ovid, Metamorphosis, Clytie, whose love for the Sun-God Helios is
unrequited, is transformed to a flower facing the sun.*

Vintage Chutney

From the worn-thin
rungs
of a wooden ladder

we examine
this year's fruit —
perfectly imperfect:

crusted, mottled,
cracked.
We clutch and twist,

drop
each apple
to a shoulder sack.

An occasional
sideways glance
to smile at an odd shape

we work
through the afternoon's
amber light

until 5 o'clock,
then peel and cut,
simmer

two old pans;
this year's onions,
tomatoes and spice.

Quiet hours
of stirring and waiting,
the scent of it...

Yellow Leaves

I was looking at an old sycamore
for about an hour, maybe longer.

I saw green, fresh as a field after rain,
lime, almost ripe, and yellow.

Bright as sunlight, dry and weightless,
the yellow leaves started to fall away.

I never heard a snap,
I never heard anything.

For a moment they sat on air,
then dropped casually to soft earth.

That's how I want to go,
like a yellow leaf.

The Ride Home

She escapes a city's insistent pulse,
its harsh inequity, its critique laid bare
in so many closed conversations.
She craves the silence of field and sky,
winter trees; only her breathing,
a few dry leaves lifted from a clay path.
This woman is neither lonely, nor sad;
rather, in the quiet joy of solitude,
free of her daily work, a silhouette,
pedalling into the sun's fire.

It's always here, this tall sycamore,
a rooted giant in amber light.
If she knew the language of trees,
she'd ask if it could feel the changing weather,
how it learned to flex in a storm.
Of its circular life, she'd ask if leaves
fell willingly when it was time,
and was it certain of greening every year.
In the minutes before sunset,
she imagines the sycamore answers.

Two Sisters

Blown in by a salt wind,
one across the water, the other
from Donegal, they stand
on the western shore
searching each other's eyes
behind surprising lines.

A quiet embrace for the heart,
a flash-back to ponytails and bicycles,
before the rising brume
of love and duty,
to husbands and children,
to God.

Shadow-lives
cast in heritage and prayer,
too early to share
the ripening fruit of tutored minds,
the talk of art and literature,
or European tours.

Old men, who in their turn
were taught to build
their low and narrow space,
now learn from their daughters,
Irish women in full flight,
erudite and free.

In the hour before sunset,
two sisters call again
to wild, silver waves,
remember their joy,
running, laughing, falling
on grubby knees.

A Distant Field

Beyond this grave, its single rose,
the three-railed, ashen fence,
beyond hushed woodland,
folds of valley and stream

a field breathes under the harrow.
From hay bales and blackthorn,
September shadows lean
to its hessian weave.

Your narrow path through the field
is barely visible,
melting away in day-light hours
like spent dreams.

On warm air and taut wings,
ravens circle again,
soundless in silhouette, they wait
high above the naked soil.

Dust clouds lift and fall;
bird song, faltering now,
frames the evening quiet
until a cockerel calls in the night.

Imagining Angels

When he saw Da Vinci's Vitruvian Man
with its perfect ratio and proportion,
he thought he might resemble
an early maquette, to be cast aside.

Older now, he knows beauty in all things,
exactly as they are — their imperfections,
preferring instead the unfettered
geometry of circumstance.

He has taken soundings of his life,
recalled the tears of things:
pain, loss, grief, as well as joy
found in the ordinary

and realised he needs to keep
imagining angels rooted to earth,
to the old or the broken,
living quietly with us and within us.

Paradox is easier to understand:
how we can be both fragile and resilient,
humble and yet powerful,
our wings lifted, ready to embrace.

Acknowledgements

I would like to thank the members of Louth Writing Groups and Nunsthorpe Poets for their encouragement and constructive critique. Particular thanks goes to the poet, Robert Etty, Ian Gouge at Coverstory books, and to my good friend and mentor, Paul Sutherland.

I would also like to thank Denise Doherty who inspired me to write, and my partner, Sheri Young, for her help with editing and her endless patience.

- 'Aftermath' was first published in *Dream Catcher*, 2021
- 'A Borrowed Feast' and 'Alcock Tarn' were first published in *The Dawntreader*, 2021
- 'American Dream' was first published in *The Ekphrastic Review*, 2021
- 'In Praise of Sunflower Leaves', 'The End of Something' and 'The River Welcomes Strangers' were first published in *Reach Poetry*, 2021
- 'Lost' was first published in *Spelt*, 2021
- 'The Old Masters' was first published in *Acumen*, 2021
- 'A Small Triumph', 'Two Sisters' and 'Gold Watch and a Badge' were first published in *Reach Poetry*, 2022
- 'Last Fall' was first published in *The Dawntreader*. 2022
- 'The January Tree' was first published in *Black Bough*, 2022
- 'The Oarsman and the Swan' was first published in *The Dawntreader*, 2023
- 'An Extraordinary, Ordinary Man', 'First year', 'From a Bench', 'Legacy' and 'On Reflection' were first published in *Reach Poetry*, 2023
- 'Christmas Eve' was first published in *Black Bough*, 2023
- 'Resurrection', 'To Siobahn', 'The Loneliness Thing is Overdone' and 'Five Days' were first published in *The High Window*, 2023
- 'That Bloody Book' was first published in *George Orwell Studies*, 2024
- 'Ode to Joy', 'A Sense' and 'Returning Alone to Glebe Farm' were first published in *Reach Poetry*, 2024
- 'A Distant Field' was first published in *Acumen*, 2024
- 'Imagining Angels', 'The Ride Home', '+2.5∘C', 'Tien Shan' and 'Spring Watch' were first published in *Littoral Magazine*, 2025
- 'A Rare and Precious Thing' was first published in *Reach Poetry*, 2025
- 'Nymphéas' will be published in *The Dawntreader*, 2025